A Tiny Flower, Lent not Given

A Journey Through The Loss Of Your Baby

Helen Pugh

Copyright © *Helen Pugh,* 2024
All Rights Reserved

This book is subject to the condition that no part of this book is to be reproduced, transmitted in any form or means; electronic or mechanical, stored in a retrieval system, photocopied, recorded, scanned, or otherwise. Any of these actions require the proper written permission of the author.

In Loving Memory of Matthew
His brief but profound presence will be forever cherished in my heart and memories.

23rd January 1990 -
25th January 1990

"A tiny flower, lent not given, to bud on earth and bloom in heaven"

IN MEMORY OF

NAME ....
DATE ....
WEIGHT ....
HAIR COLOUR ....

A Tiny Flower, Lent Not Given

I sincerely hope that this book can offer comfort and companionship to parents who are journeying through the heartache of losing their beloved baby.

It's my aspiration that within these pages, you'll find a haven for contemplation, a sanctuary for healing, and a gentle embrace for remembering the precious moments shared with your little one.

My own experience with loss, like that of my son Matthew, who graced this world for only two days after being born prematurely at 28 weeks, has taught me that the ache of such a profound loss is unfathomable to those who haven't walked this path.

Amidst well-meaning advice that often falls short in the face of such grief, it's natural to feel isolated in that vast emptiness.

I hope that through the words in this book, you might discover something that resonates, something that offers a glimmer of solace amidst the darkness.

Remember, you are not alone in your journey of healing and remembrance.

Table of Contents

Introduction	9
The Early Days	12
Leaving the Hospital	14
The Mountain	16
How Should I Feel	23
Looking After Yourself Through the Grieving Process	26
Registering Baby's Birth & Death	44
Saying Goodbye	45
After Your Baby's Farewell	48
Well-Meaning yet Hurtful Words:	
The Challenge of Unsolicited Advice and Comments	53
Managing Your Grief in Everyday Life	58
Returning to Work After the Loss of Your Baby	63
Special Dates	72
Relationships After Baby Loss	80
Whispers of Love	85
Memory Box	86
How Many Children Do You Have?	90
Being Around Babies	92
Pregnant Friends and Family	97

Has Everyone Forgotten and Moved On?	106
Your Story	111
Having Another Baby	117
Forever Remembered	122
Matthew's Story	123
A Journey to Freedom	131
Tiny Light	132
Matthew's Eternal Light	133
Keeping Baby's Memory Alive	137
Help and Support	144

INTRODUCTION

Losing a baby is an experience that shatters the very foundation of your world, leaving you grappling with a pain that defies words.

In the aftermath of such a devastating loss, there is no rule book to turn to, no guide to navigate the labyrinth of grief. Every moment becomes a maze of uncertainty, each step forward fraught with the weight of sorrow and longing.

You find yourself adrift in a sea of emotions, struggling to make sense of a reality that feels utterly incomprehensible. There are no prescribed paths to follow, no timelines for healing; instead, there is only the relentless ache of an empty crib, the haunting echo of a lullaby that will never be sung.

Yet, amidst the darkness, there is a flicker of hope – a glimmer of resilience that whispers of the possibility of finding light in the midst of despair.

And so, you embark on a journey of healing, guided not by rules or expectations, but by the enduring love you hold for your little baby, whose memory will forever be etched upon your hearts.

Love's Everlasting Embrace

In the silence of your grief's
embrace, Know you're not
alone in this space.
Though shadows loom and
fears may rise, Love's
presence never fades or dies.

UNKNOWN

If there ever comes a day when we can't be together. Keep me in your heart, I'll stay there forever.

POOH BEAR

THE EARLY DAYS

The early days following the loss of a baby are often filled with an overwhelming mix of emotions, each one intense and raw. There's a profound sense of shock and disbelief, as the reality of the loss sinks in. Many parents find themselves cycling through waves of intense grief, anger, guilt, and profound sadness. Simple daily tasks may feel insurmountable, as the weight of sorrow hangs heavy in the air.

Physically, there may be lingering reminders of the pregnancy or birth, adding an extra layer of pain to the emotional turmoil. Sleepless nights and exhaustion become constant companions, as the mind replays the events leading up to the loss, searching for answers that may never come.

Amidst the grief, there's also a sense of isolation—a feeling that the world continues to spin while yours has come to a standstill. Friends and family may offer well-meaning words of comfort, but it's hard to find solace in their presence when the ache of loss feels all-consuming.

In the midst of this darkness, there can also be moments of unexpected grace—a gentle touch, a shared memory, or a kind word that offers a glimmer of light in the darkness.

Though the pain may feel unbearable, there's a sense of resilience that begins to take root—a quiet strength that allows parents to take each day as it comes, finding small moments of peace amidst the storm.

Above all, the early days after baby loss are a journey through the depths of grief—a journey that no one should have to take alone. It's a time for self-compaassion, for seeking support, and for honoring the love that will forever live on in the hearts of those who grieve.

LEAVING THE HOSPITAL
My Experience

Although Matthew's passing was many years ago, returning home from the hospital without him was a memory I will never forget. The journey marked by a profound sense of emptiness. As I walked through the sterile corridors of the hospital, the weight of grief hung heavy around my shoulders, pressing down with every step. Each door I passed through seemed to close behind me with a finality that echoed the emptiness in my arms.

The drive home was a blur of tears and numbness, the world outside the window passing by in a haze. The streets I had travelled countless times before now felt unfamiliar, as if I were navigating a foreign landscape. The silence of the car was deafening, broken only by the occasional sob that escaped from deep within me.

Arriving home felt like stepping into a void, a place where the absence of my baby loomed large in every corner. The unused baby items lovingly chosen, once filled with anticipation and hope, now stood as a stark reminder of the dreams that would never be realised.

The presence of family and friends reminded me that I was not alone in my grief, that there were others who shared in my pain and were willing to walk alongside me on this journey.

In my darkest moments, my Nan was the unwavering pillar of strength I leaned on, her love and resilience guided me through the storms of grief.

THE MOUNTAIN

If the mountain seems too big today
then climb a hill instead;
If morning brings you sadness
it's okay to stay in bed.
If the day ahead feels heavy and your plans feel
like a curse,
There's no shame in rearranging,
don't make yourself feel worse.
If a shower stings like needles
and a bath feels like you'll drown;
If you haven't washed your hair for days,
don't throw away your crown!
A day is not a lifetime.
A rest is not defeat.
Don't think of it as failure,
Just a quiet, kind retreat.
It's okay to take a moment
From an anxious, fractured mind.
The world will not stop turning
While you get realigned!
The mountain will still be there
When you want to try again
You can climb it in your own time,
Just love yourself till then!

LAURA DING-EDWARDS

Write about your baby's name, if given, and what it means to you. If you didn't name your baby, consider choosing a name now and reflect on its significance.

Use the following pages to write letters to your baby expressing your love, grief, and longing. What would you want your baby to know?

Letters to my baby.

Letters to my baby.

Letters to my baby.

Letters to my baby.

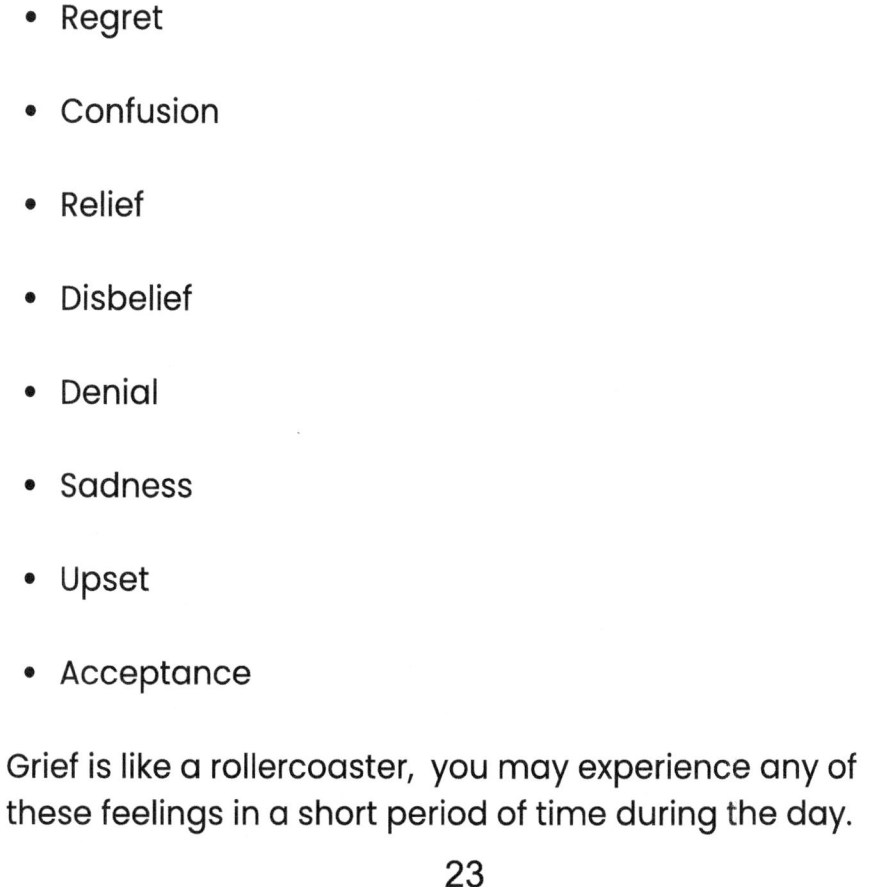

HOW SHOULD I FEEL?

It's OK to feel all of these things and anything else you may feel.

- Shock
- Worry
- Anger
- Guilt
- Regret
- Confusion
- Relief
- Disbelief
- Denial
- Sadness
- Upset
- Acceptance

Grief is like a rollercoaster, you may experience any of these feelings in a short period of time during the day.

You may have no clue how you feel from one minute to the next. You may have lots of physical reactions too:

- Headaches

- Sleeping issues – too much or not enough

- nausea

- Upset stomach

- Lack of interest in anything

- Outbursts of anger or frustration

- Feelings of panic

- Feeling numb

- Nightmares

And many more things, if you are concerned, it is important that you reach out to your doctor.

Let's reflect upon how you are feeling at the moment.

LOOKING AFTER YOURSELF THROUGH THE GRIEVING PROCESS

Looking after yourself while grieving is crucial for navigating through the emotional turmoil. Firstly, be gentle with yourself and acknowledge that grieving is a natural process that takes time.

Prioritise self-care activities that nourish your mind, body, and soul. This could include getting enough rest, eating nourishing foods, and engaging in regular physical activity to help manage stress.

Express your emotions in healthy ways, whether through journaling, talking to a trusted friend or therapist, or engaging in creative outlets like art or music. Establishing a routine can provide a sense of stability amidst the chaos of grief.

Be mindful of your boundaries and give yourself permission to say no to additional responsibilities if needed. Seek support from loved ones or support groups who can offer understanding and companionship along the journey. Remember, healing takes time, so be patient with yourself and allow yourself to grieve in your own way.

As time goes by, the individuals who offer you support and the methods you employ to navigate through the days, weeks, and months will likely become ingrained coping mechanisms.

Writing down these triggers and coping strategies can heighten your awareness. and provide clarity on who to turn to when you feel overwhelmed. Everyone will be different and there is no right answer.

Your triggers may be a certain song, seeing families together. Someone elses could just be a certain smell or thinking too much about the future.

Same with your coping mechanisms. You may choose going for a long walk, having a break from social media or binge watching a series. For someone else it may be meeting with friends or taking a long bath.

The next few pages are to help you with coping mechanisms. I have included more than one page because your support circle, trigger and coping mechanisms will change over time.

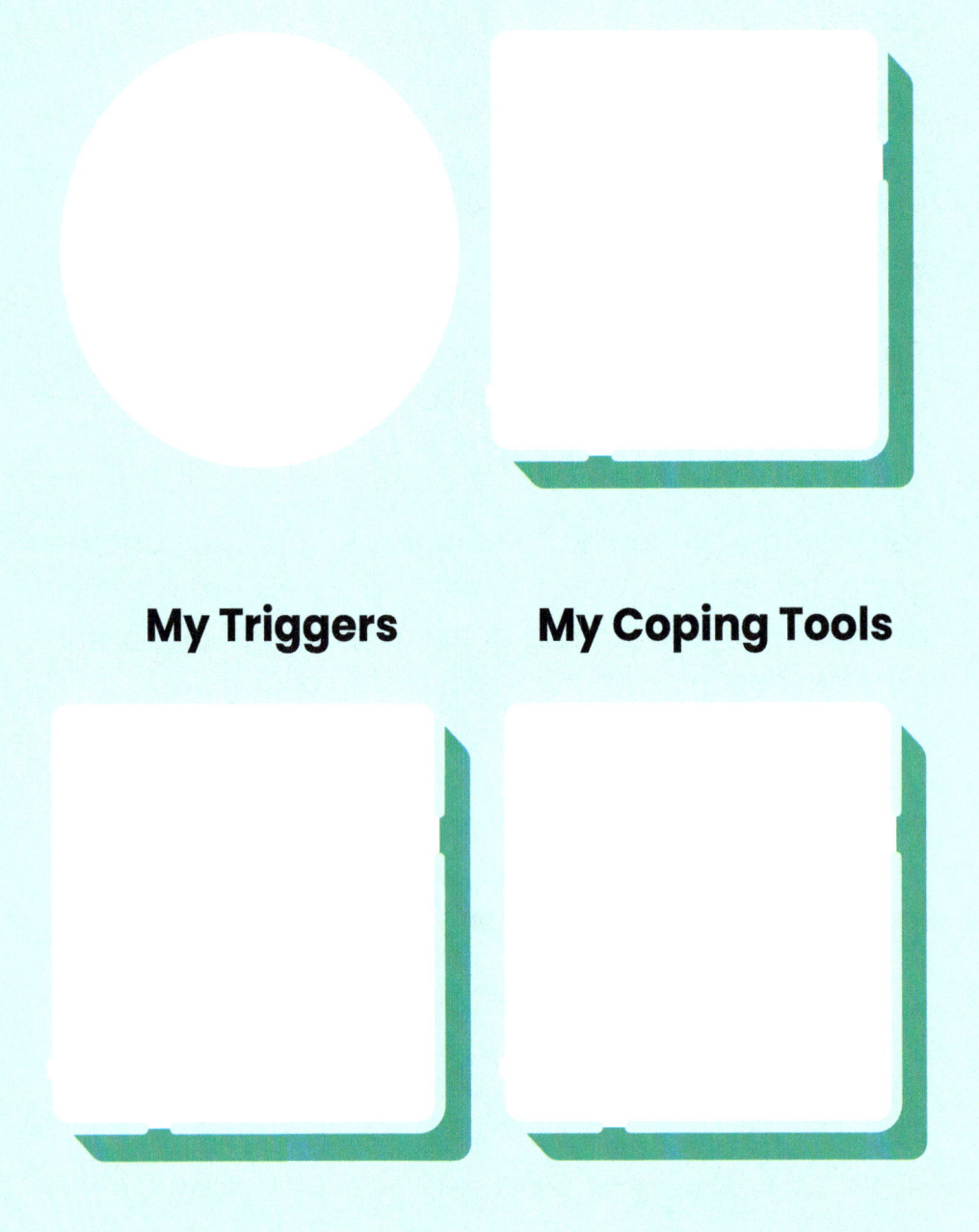

My Circle Of Support

My Triggers

My Coping Tools

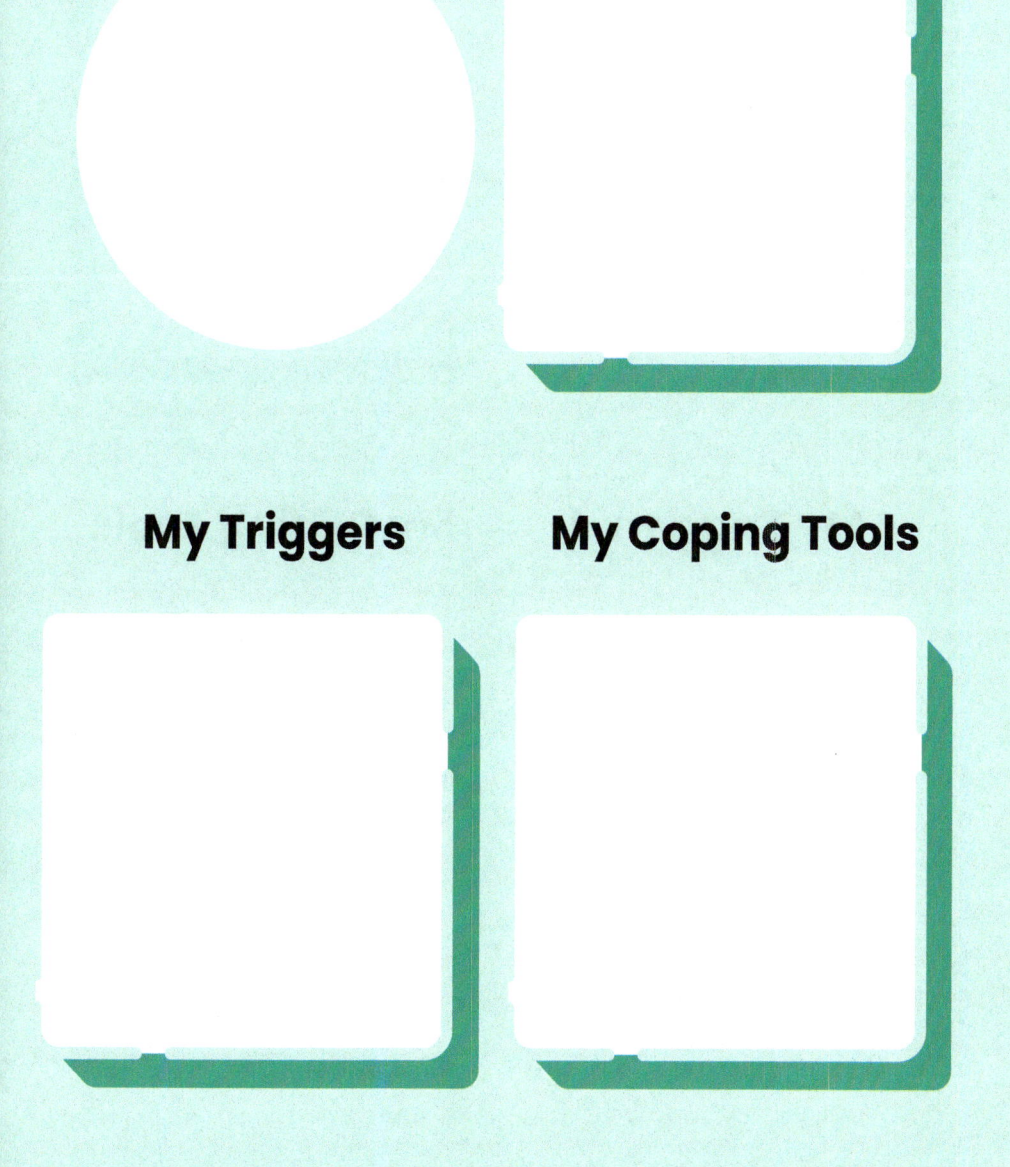

My Circle Of Support

My Triggers

My Coping Tools

My Circle Of Support

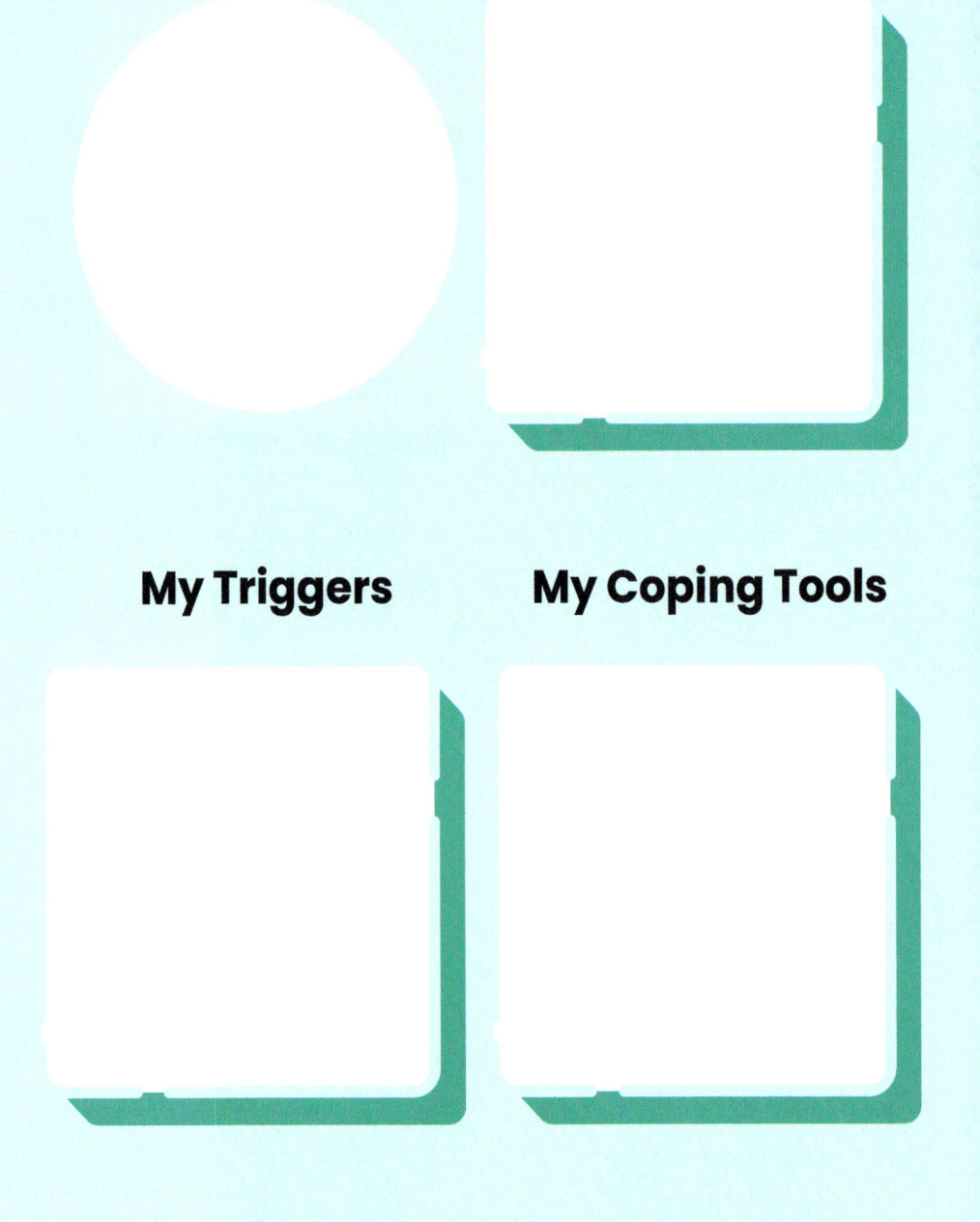

My Triggers

My Coping Tools

In times of grief, finding moments of peace and comfort can feel like a daunting task. However, simple activities can often provide solace amidst the storm.

Consider trying colouring as a gentle way to ease the burden of stress and sorrow. Engaging in this creative outlet allows you to focus your mind on soothing patterns and colours, providing a temporary respite from the weight of your emotions. It requires no special skills or equipment, just a willingness to immerse yourself in the calming rhythm of colouring.

Allow yourself the space to breathe and heal as you let the colours guide you through your journey of grief.

In the following pages, you'll find a tranquil space where you can take a brief respite from the world and fully immerse yourself in a sense of calmness.

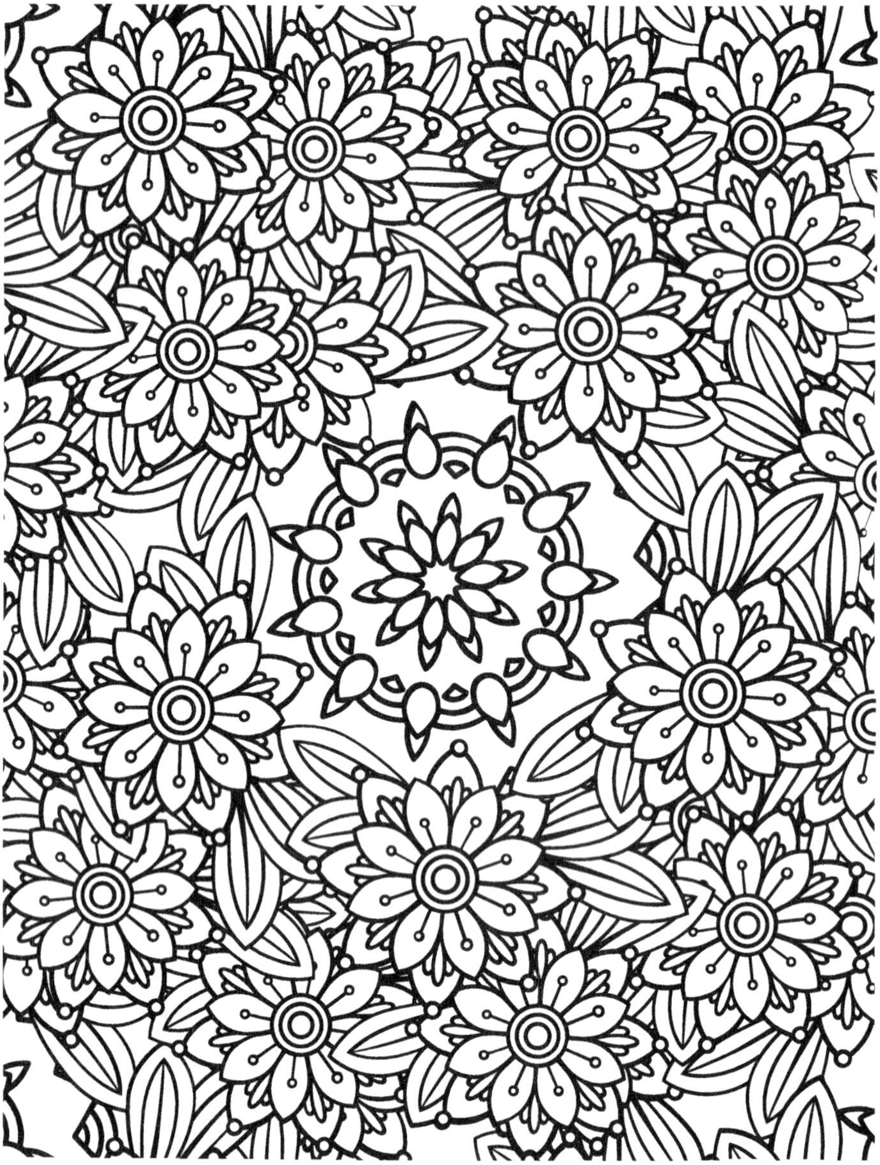

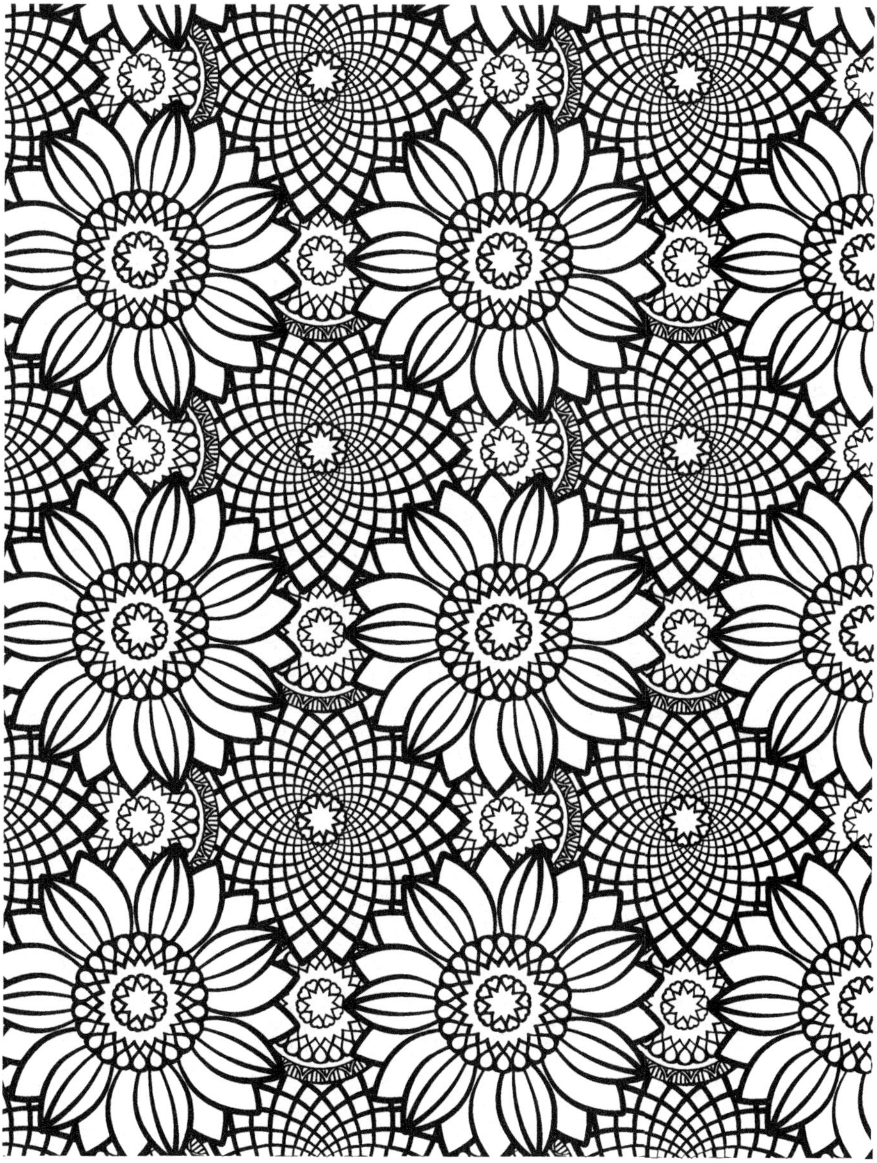

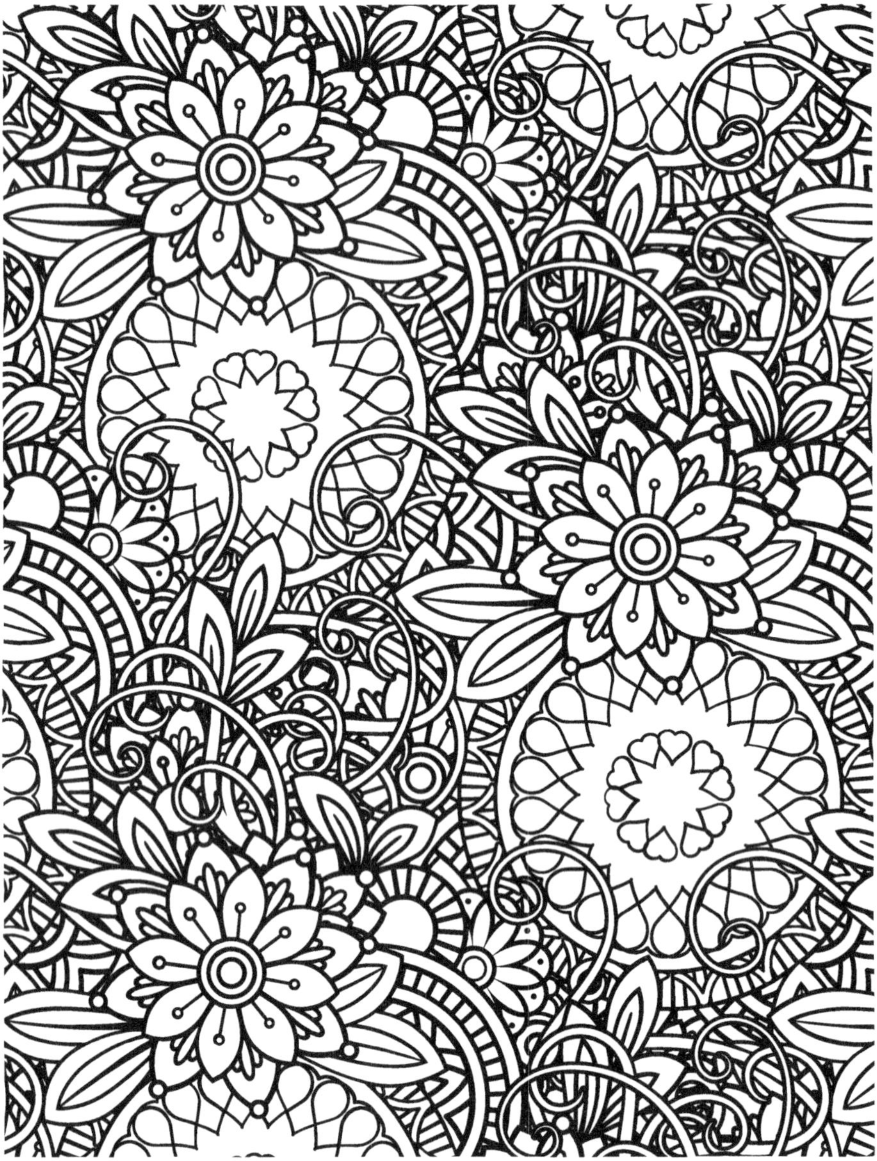

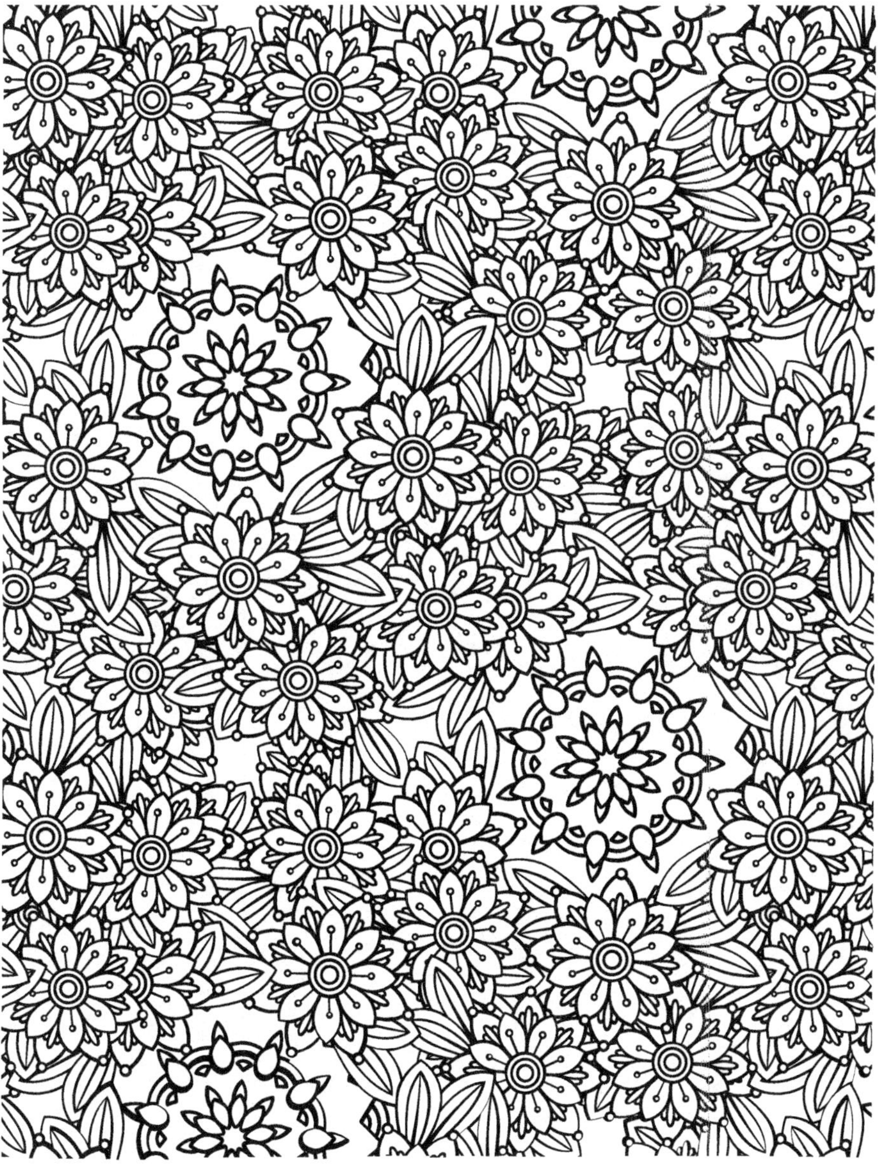

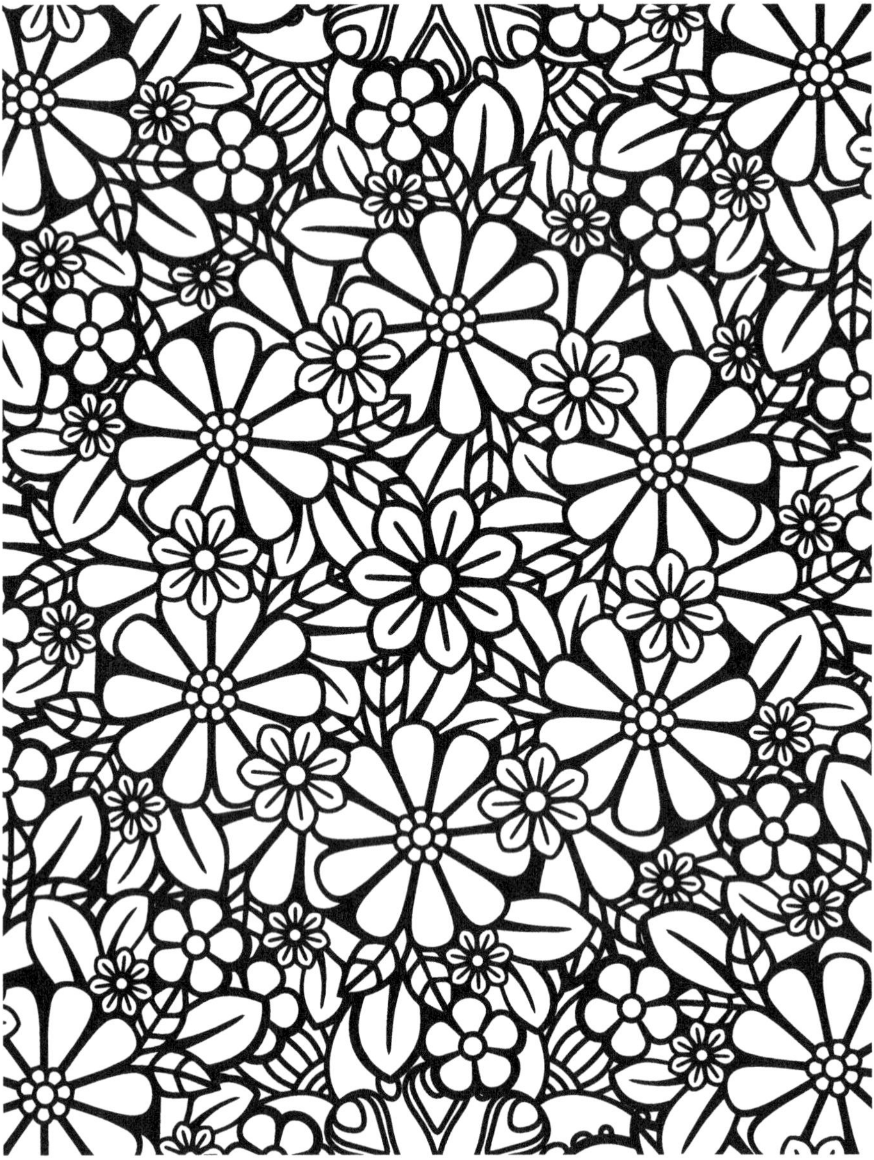

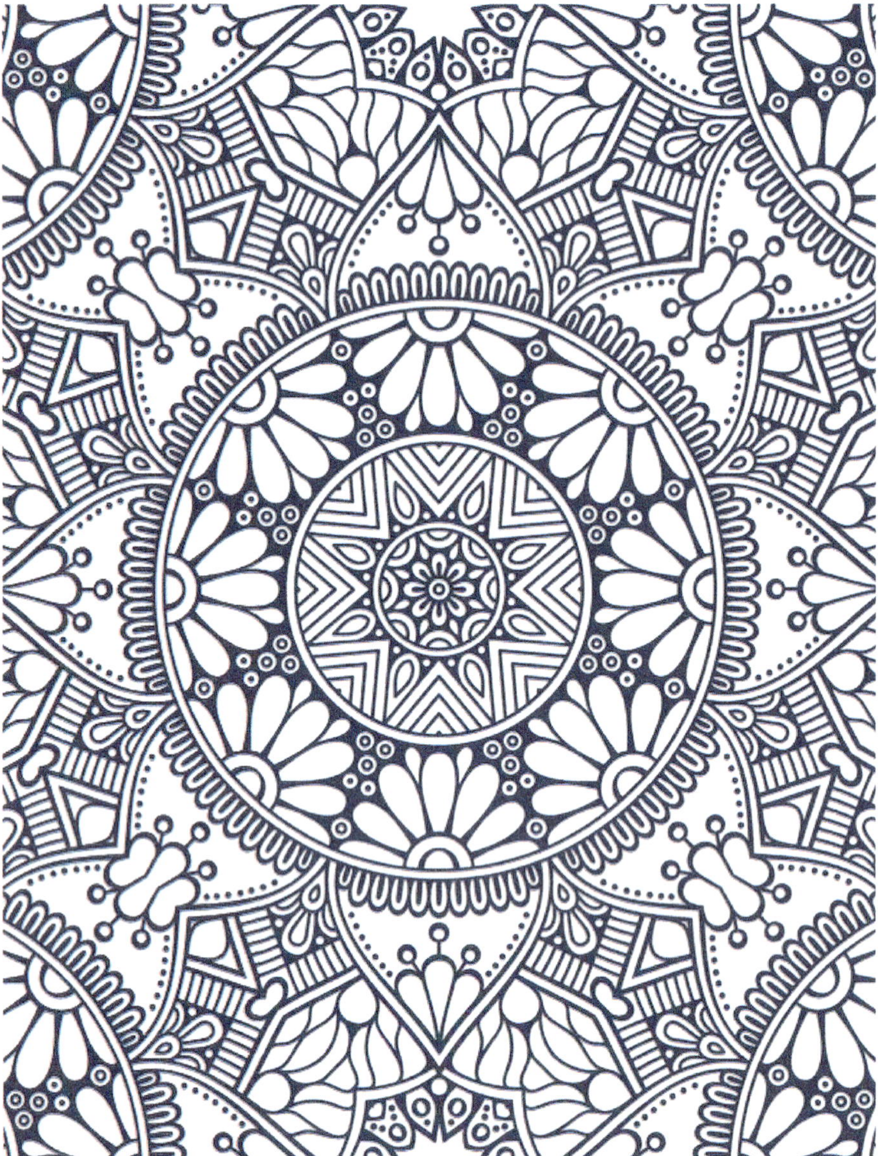

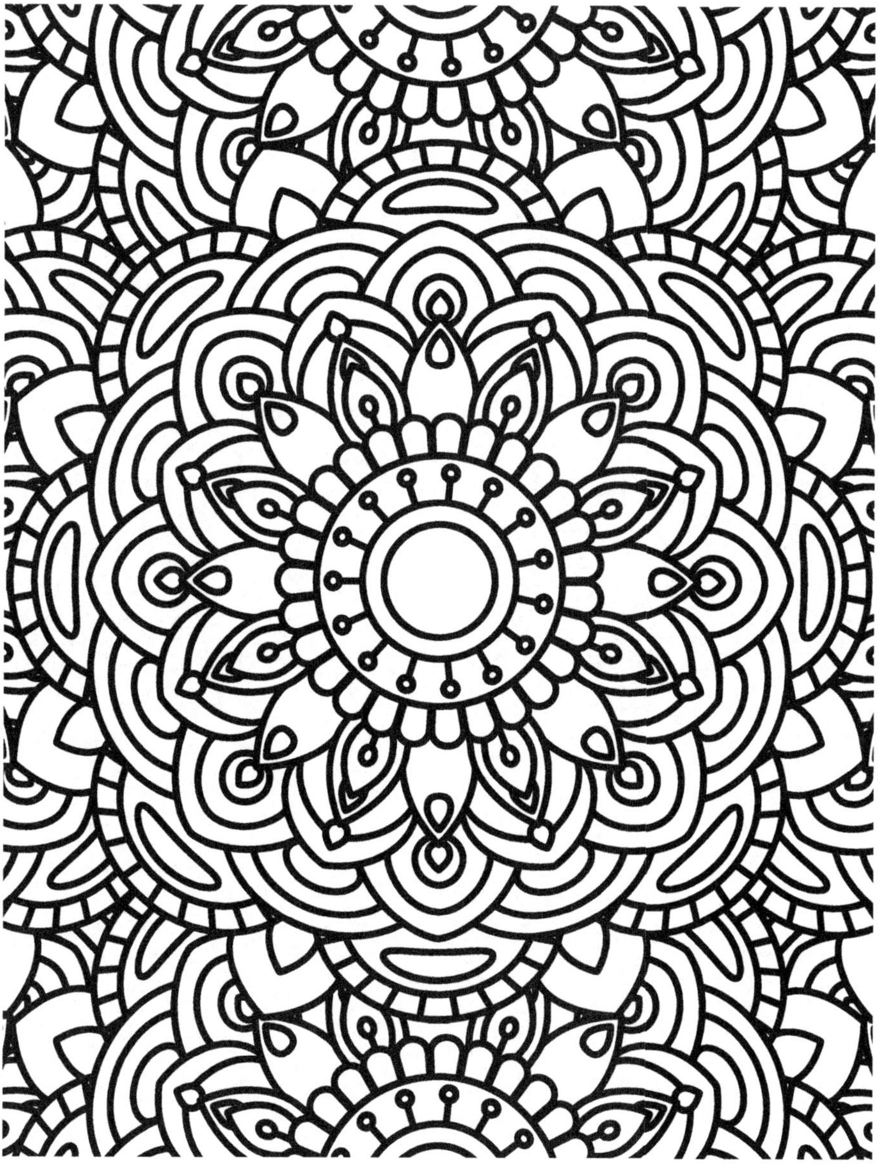

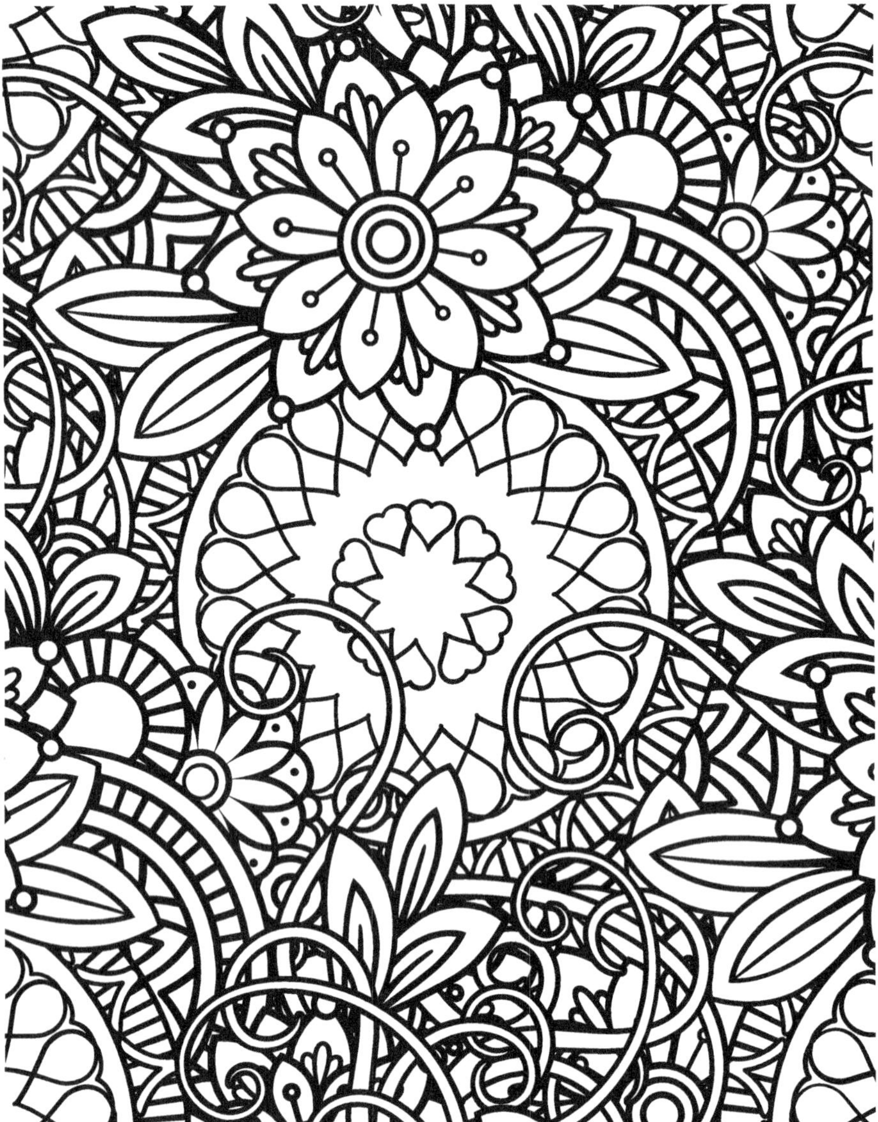

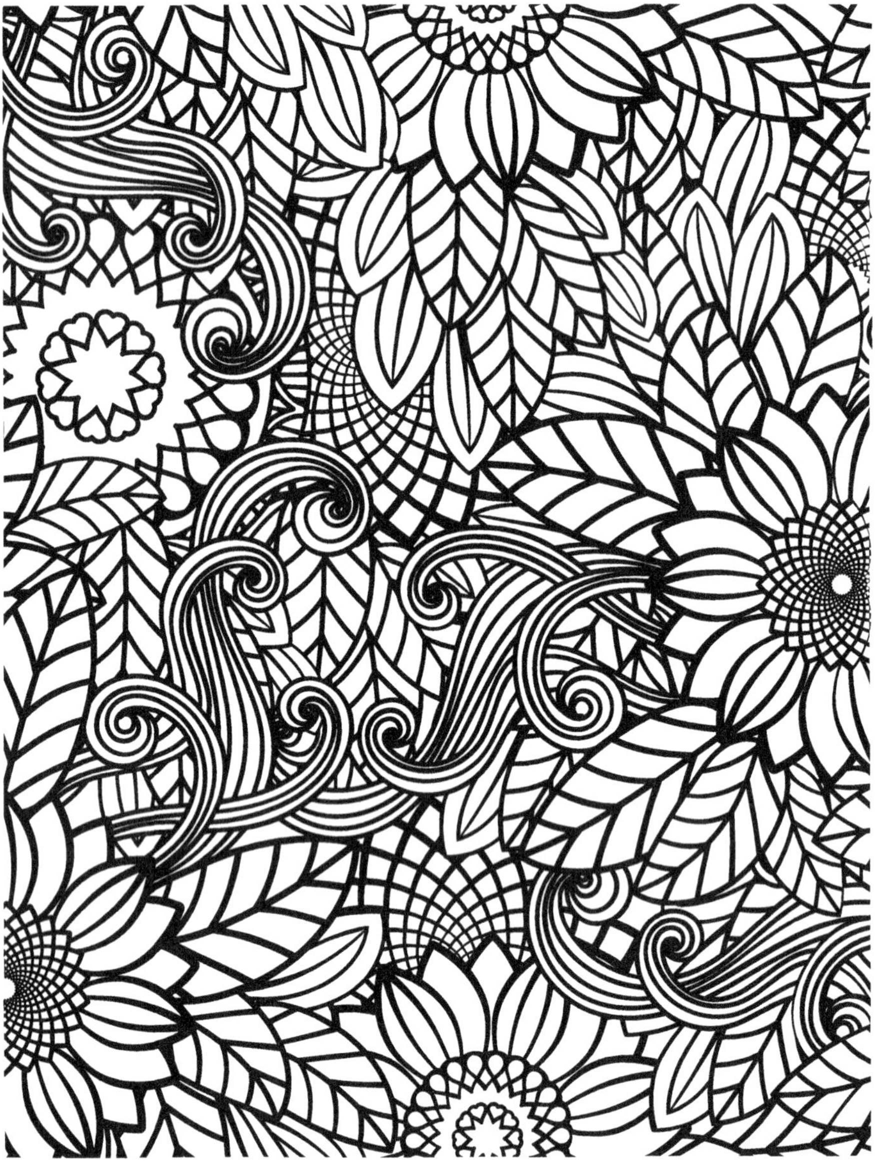

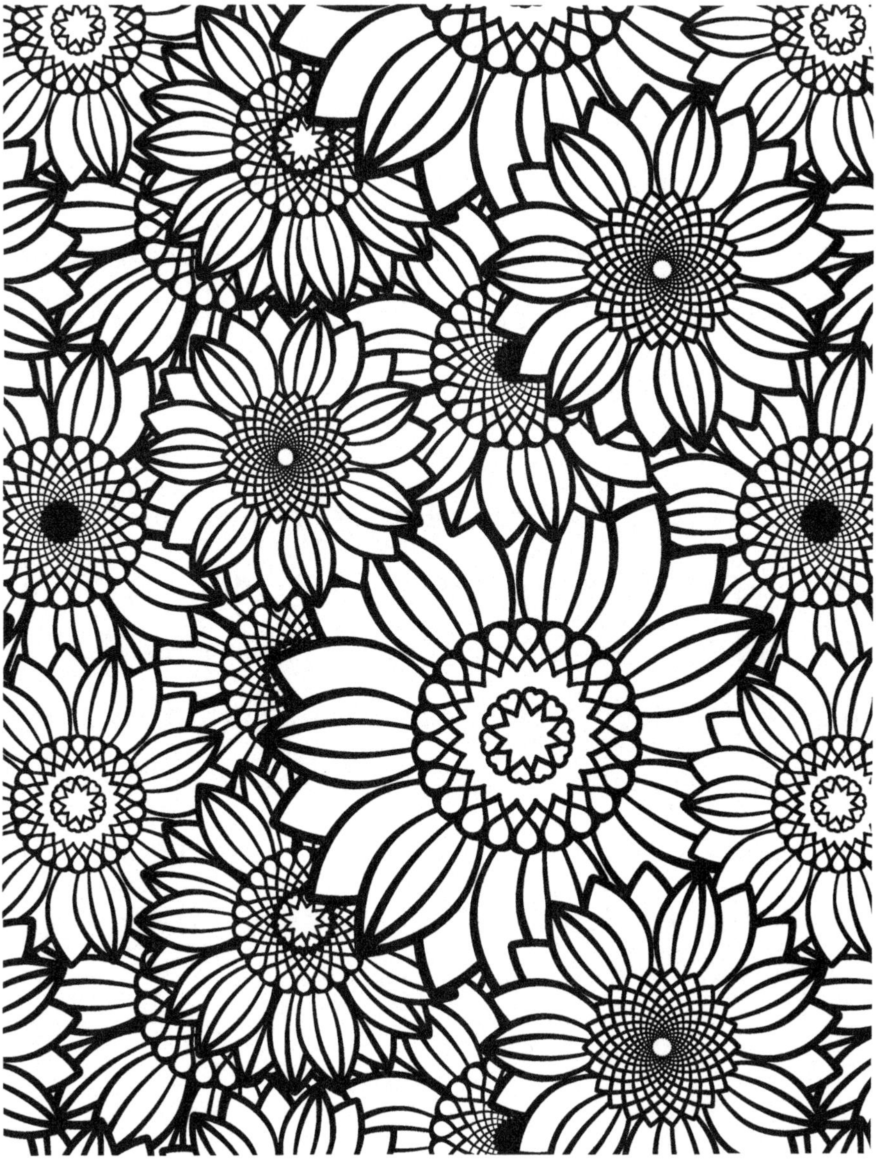

REGISTERING BABY'S BIRTH & DEATH

Registering Matthew's birth and death in a single visit was an emotionally overwhelming experience, the joy of welcoming a new life with the profound sorrow of saying goodbye. It's a stark reminder of life's fragility and the unexpected twists it can take.

The bureaucratic process of filling out forms and official documents was an agonising task, forcing us to confront the finality of Matthew's brief existence. Each signature, each acknowledgment, was a painful reminder of the hopes and dreams that would never come to fruition. I remember the registrar, being empathetic and understanding.

It's a journey no parent should ever have to endure, yet it becomes a testament to the strength and resilience of our human spirit in the face of unimaginable loss.

SAYING GOODBYE

Matthew's Farewell

While not every baby loss journey allows for a formal funeral, the ache of parting remains just as profound.

Matthew was baptised while he was in the neonatal unit. Once we had registered his birth and death, we were able to hold a funeral for him. He was laid to rest in a special area of the cemetry dedicated to babies.

In the quiet moments of Matthew's ceremony, we were able to honor his brief but impactful presence, a moment to acknowledge the depth of our love, and a moment to find solace in the memories we held dear.

Burying or cremating your baby is a deeply personal and emotional process. Families are provided with various options and support systems to ensure that they can make the best decision for their unique situation.

The emphasis on respect, dignity, and sensitivity helps families navigate this challenging experience, allowing them to honor their baby's memory in a meaningful and respectful way.

How you choose to honour your baby is personal to you. There is no right or wrong way, whether you choose a burial, somewhere you can visit or whether you choose cremation and take you baby home.   You will choose what is comforting for you.

Saying goodbye to your baby after miscarriage when a formal funeral isn't possible can still be a meaningful and healing process.

Name your baby: Give your baby a name if you haven't already. This can help to personalise your connection and provide a sense of identity.

Create a memorial: Plant a tree in their memory. Have a special candle that you light.

There is no right or wrong way to say goodbye after a miscarriage. Trust your instincts and do what feels most meaningful and healing to you and your family.

Allow yourself space to grieve and seek support when you need it, all of you.

AFTER YOUR BABY'S FAREWELL

You might find a huge dip in emotion. You might feel the following:

- Lacking motivation

- Feeling tired

- Unable to concentrate

- Unable to make decisions

- Craving to be alone

- Craving to be with people and not alone

- Feeling the the world is unfair

- Feeling lost and like you aren't in your own body.

- Wanting to lash out at everyone.

- Emotionally unstable

Use these pages to write about your baby's farewell and how it made you feel. If you weren't able to have a formal farewell, use this space to say goodbye to your baby.

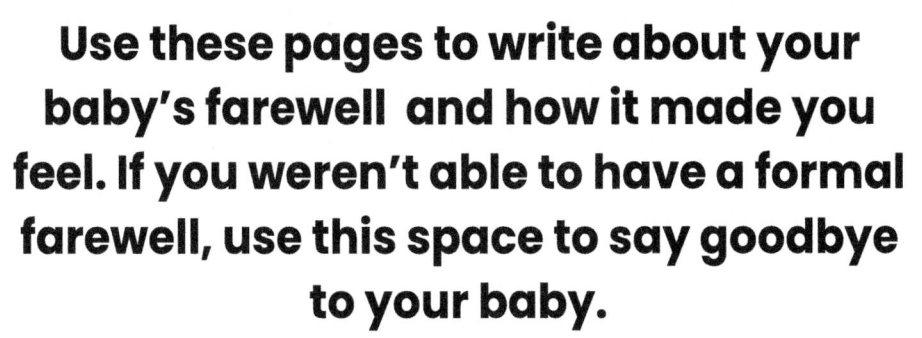

An Angel in the Book of Life wrote down my baby's birth, then whispered as she closed the book "Too beautiful for earth"

UNKNOWN

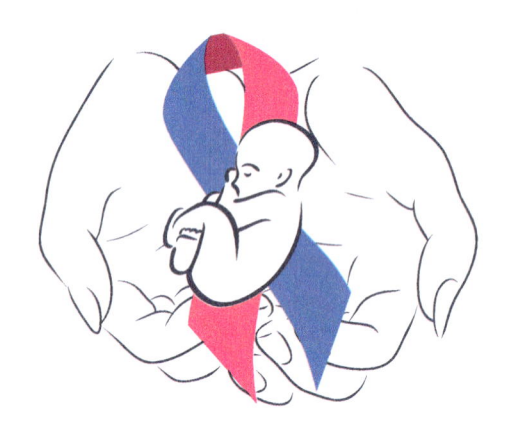

WELL-MEANING YET HURTFUL WORDS: THE CHALLENGE OF UNSOLICITED ADVICE AND COMMENTS

In the wake of losing a baby, the landscape of grief often becomes littered with well-intentioned but inadvertently hurtful words. From awkward platitudes to misguided attempts at comfort, the journey through baby loss can feel compounded by the weight of others' words.

This is some of the comments, advice, words that I heard:

"At Least you can try again"

"Everything happens for a reason"

"It's time to move on"

"You're young, you can have more babies"

"I know how you feel"

"Maybe it's for the best"

"You will get over it eventually"

"Maybe there was something wrong, and it is better this way"

"At Least it happened early, before you got to know the baby"

and
Silence and avoidance

These words can feel like people are minimising our loss, dismissing our grief and implying that we can simply replace our baby.

What we as bereaved parents truly yearn for is empathy, validation, and the simple presence of loved ones. We seek understanding without judgment, a safe space to express our emotions freely, and the reassurance that our grief is seen and acknowledged.

In these moments of profound pain, the greatest gift friends and family can offer is a compassionate ear, a tender shoulder to lean on, and unwavering support through the darkest of days. It's not about finding the right words to say, but rather about being there with an open heart, ready to listen, to hold space, and to walk alongside us on our journey of healing.

Use these pages to pour out your feelings when someone has said or done something that has upset you.

MANAGING YOUR GRIEF IN EVERYDAY LIFE

Handling your grief while managing work, daily chores, and other commitments can be immensely challenging. The weight of grief can make even the simplest tasks feel overwhelming. Here are some common difficulties you may encounter and strategies for coping:

Lack of Concentration: Grief can cloud your mind, making it difficult to concentrate on work tasks or even remember simple chores. You may find yourself easily distracted or unable to focus for extended periods.

Fatigue and Low Energy: The emotional toll of grief can leave you feeling physically exhausted, making it hard to muster the energy needed to fulfill work responsibilities or keep up with household tasks.

Emotional Overload: Grieving often involves intense emotions that can surface unexpectedly throughout the day. These emotions may interfere with your ability to function effectively in your professional and personal life.

Difficulty Prioritising: When you're grieving, it can be challenging to prioritise tasks and responsibilities. You may struggle to determine which tasks are most urgent or important, leading to feelings of overwhelm.

Balancing Self-Care with Obligations: Taking care of yourself is crucial during grief, but it can feel selfish or indulgent when there are work deadlines to meet and household chores to complete. Finding the balance between self-care and fulfilling obligations can be difficult.

To cope with these challenges, it's important to be gentle with yourself and acknowledge that it's okay to struggle. Here are some strategies that may help:

- **Set Realistic Expectations:** Recognise that you may not be able to perform at your usual level while grieving. Set realistic expectations for yourself and prioritise essential tasks while letting go of perfectionism.

- **Break Tasks into Smaller Steps:** If tasks feel too overwhelming, break them down into smaller, more manageable steps. Focus on completing one small task at a time rather than trying to tackle everything at once.

- **Communicate with Others:** Don't hesitate to communicate your needs to your employer, colleagues, and loved ones. Let them know that you're grieving and may need some flexibility or support during this time.

- **Schedule Time for Self-Care:** Make self-care a priority by scheduling time for activities that nourish your mind, body, and soul. Whether it's taking a walk in, practicing meditation, or spending time with loved ones, prioritise activities that bring you comfort and solace.

- **Seek Professional Support:** Consider seeking support from a therapist or counsellor who can provide guidance and coping strategies tailored to your unique situation. Professional support can be invaluable in navigating the challenges of grief while managing everyday life.

Remember, grief is a deeply personal experience, and there is no right or wrong way to grieve. Be patient with yourself as you navigate this difficult journey, and remember that healing takes time.

Managing Grief in Everyday Life: Write about your difficulties in handling your grief while juggling work, daily chores, and other commitments.

RETURNING TO WORK AFTER THE LOSS OF YOUR BABY

Returning to work after experiencing the loss of a baby is a journey that intertwines grief with the demands of professional life. It is a path marked by both resilience and vulnerability, where the steps forward often feel tentative and uncertain. Here is a reflection on this delicate transition:

Returning to work after the loss of a baby is one of the most challenging experiences a person can face. The grief is still raw, a constant undercurrent to every waking moment, and the thought of resuming a routine can be overwhelming. Yet, there comes a time when stepping back into the professional world is a necessary part of the healing process, a step towards finding a new normal.

The first day back is often the hardest. Walking into the workplace, it feels as though an invisible barrier has been crossed—one that separates the 'before' from the 'after.' The familiar surroundings, once a place of productivity and purpose, now feel alien, almost intrusive. Colleagues may approach with sympathy, their eyes reflecting a mixture of compassion and uncertainty, unsure of what to say or how to act. Their well-intentioned words sometimes fall flat, and their silence can feel just as heavy.

Navigating these interactions requires immense strength. It helps to remember that their discomfort stems from a place of care. They may not have the right words, but their presence is a testament to their support. Allowing yourself to be vulnerable in these moments can foster genuine connections, even if it's just a simple acknowledgment of their sympathy with a nod or a quiet "thank you."

Work itself can be both a refuge and a challenge. On one hand, diving into tasks can provide a temporary escape from the pervasive sadness. On the other, the mind's ability to focus is often compromised by grief. Patience with oneself becomes crucial. It's okay to take breaks, to step away when the emotions become too overwhelming. Setting small, manageable goals for each day can help rebuild a sense of accomplishment and control.

Balancing professional responsibilities with personal healing is an ongoing process. It's important to communicate with supervisors and colleagues about what you're comfortable with and what you need. This might mean requesting flexible hours, taking on a different workload, or simply having someone to check in with regularly. Open dialogue can pave the way for a more supportive work environment, one where your needs are respected and understood.

Self-care outside of work hours becomes even more vital. Finding moments of peace and activities that bring solace, whether it's through nature walks, writing, or spending time with loved ones, can help replenish your emotional reserves. Seeking professional counselling or joining support groups can also provide a safe space to process your grief.

The journey back to work after baby loss is deeply personal and unique to each individual. There is no right or wrong way to navigate it. Allow yourself to grieve, to heal, and to find your rhythm at your own pace. With time, patience, and support, it's possible to rediscover a sense of purpose and to honor your loss while moving forward.

There might be an option for a phased return to work, but you may feel that diving back into your new normal all at once is what you need.

Returning to work after such a loss is never easy, but with compassion for yourself and the support of those around you, it is possible to find your way back to a fulfilling and meaningful professional life.

Write about how you feel about your return to work and what your concerns are.

Write about how your first day back to work felt.

"There is no footprint too small to leave an imprint on this world"

UNKNOWN

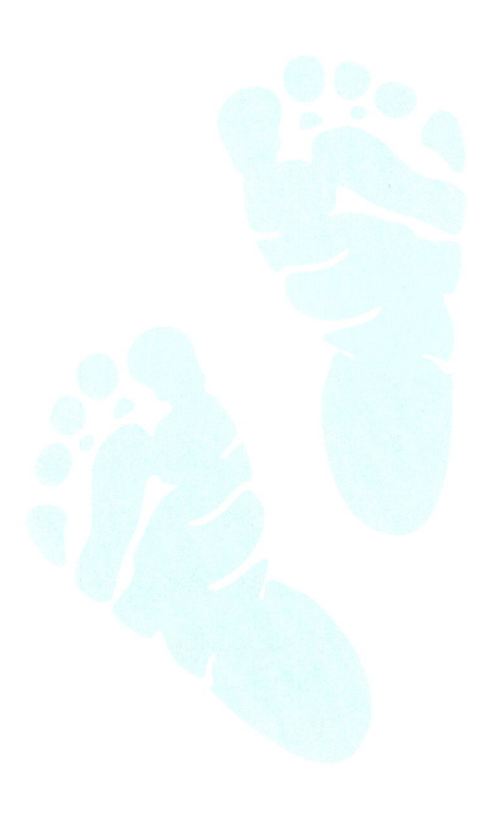

Write about the first moment you held your baby in your arms.

You were born silent,
perfect and beautiful.
Still loved
Still missed
Still remembered everyday
Stillborn but still born

UNKNOWN

SPECIAL DATES

In the initial 12 months following the loss of your baby, you may encounter numerous significant occasions and important dates that could evoke emotional responses. It's important to be mindful of these dates, including:

- Birthday
- Due Date
- Anniversary
- Mothers Day
- Fathers Day
- Baby Loss Awareness Day
- Christmas (other celebrations that bring families together)

Go into these key dates with an open mind on how you may feel. Know that if you cry, that is perfectly fine. If you feel nothing, that is also perfectly fine.

You may want to honour these dates. These are a few things that might help:

- Light a candle on these days.
- Buy a special Christmas decoration that you can hang on the tree each year. You might want to have your baby's name on and date of birth.
- Plant a Tree.

Experiencing that first Christmas after Matthew's loss was incredibly tough and deeply emotional. It seemed like every little thing, even my niece's 1st birthday just before Christmas, made me miss Matthew even more. The pain, the emptiness, and the longing felt overwhelming, and it seemed like they lingered long past the holiday season and well into February.

Christmas itself was a poignant reminder that we were nearing Matthew's 1st birthday and the anniversary of his passing. In truth, it took many years before I could truly embrace the joy of Christmas celebrations again.

Think about any significant dates coming up and what they will mean to you.

Write a Christmas Message to your baby

Write a Birthday Message to your baby

"From the briefest whispers of existence, they leave an eternal imprint of love on our souls, reminding us that even in loss, their presence is forever felt."

UNKNOWN

RELATIONSHIPS AFTER BABY LOSS

Navigating relationships after experiencing the loss of a baby can be an incredibly delicate journey for you. You and your partner may process grief differently, leading to potential misunderstandings and feelings of isolation. Communication is so important as you navigate through your individual grief while also supporting each other.

It's essential for you both to create a safe space for open dialogue, allowing you to express your emotions without judgment or expectation.

Patience, empathy, and understanding are crucial as you both learn to cope with your loss and find ways to lean on each other for strength and comfort.

Seeking professional support or joining support groups can also provide additional guidance and validation as you navigate this challenging time together.

Ultimately, by acknowledging and respecting each other's grief experiences, you can gradually rebuild your connection and find solace in your shared love and memories of your baby.

GRANDPARENTS

The loss of a grandchild can profoundly impact grandparents, as they often share a deep bond and connection with the child and their parents.

For many grandparents, the loss may evoke feelings of profound sadness, grief, and helplessness. They may experience a range of emotions, including shock, disbelief, anger, and profound sorrow.

Additionally, grandparents may also grapple with their role in supporting their own children who are grieving the loss of their baby.

It can be challenging for grandparents to find ways to offer comfort and support to their children while also managing their own grief.

The loss may also trigger memories of their own experiences with parenthood and confront them with their mortality. Some grandparents may seek solace in connecting with other family members or support groups who have experienced similar losses.

In summary, the effects of baby loss on grandparents highlight the importance of family ties and the necessity for mutual support and empathy during moments of deep grief.

SIBLINGS

The experience of baby grief can significantly affect your other children, often leading to a range of emotional responses and challenges.

Your children may feel confusion, sadness, and a sense of loss, even if they were too young to fully understand the situation.

Older children may struggle with feelings of guilt, wondering if they could have done something to prevent the loss or if they should have been able to protect their younger sibling.

Younger children might feel a sense of abandonment if you are consumed by grief and unable to provide the same level of attention and care as before.

It's essential for you to communicate openly with your children, validate their feelings, and provide them with support and reassurance during this difficult time.

Seek professional help or join support groups, this can also be beneficial for your other children as they navigate their own grief journey.

Think about how you can all continue to support one another as you continue to move forward together.

Whispers of Love

In the stillness of the night, Where stars softly gleam, I hold you close within my heart, In a world where dreams redeem.

Though your time with us was brief, Your love forever stays, In every whispered breeze that sings, In sun-kissed golden rays.

Your tiny hands, your gentle sighs, Are etched within my soul, A precious bond that time can't touch, A love that makes me whole.

Though tears may fall like gentle rain, And sorrow dims the day, Your memory shines, a guiding light, To lead us on our way.

So sleep, sweet angel, in peace profound, In Heaven's embrace, you'll stay, And in the garden of our hearts, Your love will bloom each day.

Until we meet again, my dear, Where heaven's rivers flow, You'll be the star that guides my path, The love that I'll always know.

Memory Box

A Baby Loss memory box is a gentle sanctuary filled with tender tokens and heartfelt memories.

It's a safe space where you can gather tiny treasures and precious keepsakes to honor the little one you hold in your hearts.

Inside, you might put soft blankets and tiny clothes, perhaps a lock of hair or tiny footprints, all lovingly gathered to cherish the fleeting moments you had together.

Opening a Baby Loss memory box is like wrapping ourselves in a warm embrace of love, where each item holds a piece of our precious angel's spirit, guiding us through the tender moments of remembrance.

Memory bears and blankets are also beautiful keepsakes, made out of clothing you bought for your baby.

Matthew's Memory Box

Matthew's memory box holds his tiny hat, snug from the incubator days; a soft lamb companion that kept him company. A small photo album with his baptism certificate. Cards, tokens of love from dear ones; a lock of his precious hair, and two pairs of tiny bootees, each holding a story of their own; his hospital bracelet, a silent witness to his journey; a scan picture, a glimpse into the anticipation and hope; and a tiny outfit, a gift that symbolises the love that welcomed him into this world. The items in the memory box hold immense significance to me, and I will forever cherish them close to my heart.

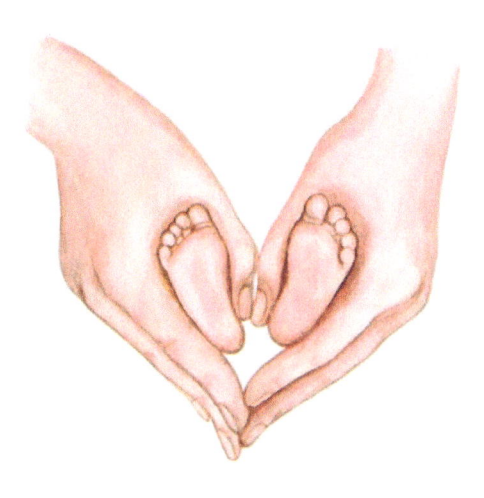

Some people like to have an area of their home or garden set aside for the memory of their baby. With photos, cuddly toys, candles or garden ornaments and a place for flowers. Not everyone understands this, this is your grief, your loss, your baby. You can hold them in your memory however you wish.

Those we have
held in our arms
for a while we hold
in our hearts
forever

Think about what you would like to do in your baby's memory.

HOW MANY CHILDREN DO YOU HAVE?

This still remains an emotionally challenging question for me, even all these years on.

Here are some strategies to consider:

Honesty: Decide how much you feel comfortable sharing with the person asking the question. You can choose to be honest about your experience and mention your angel baby along with any living children you have.

Personal Boundaries: Remember that you are not obligated to share more than you feel comfortable. It's okay to set boundaries and share only what feels right for you in that moment.

Gentle Response: Craft a gentle response that acknowledges your angel baby while also answering the question. For example, you could say, "We have one living child and we also have an angel baby who holds a special place in our hearts."

Redirect the Conversation: If you're not comfortable discussing your baby loss with the person asking the question, you can politely redirect the conversation to a different topic.

Practice Self-Care: Remember to be gentle with yourself and practice self-care after navigating such a sensitive question. Surround yourself with supportive loved ones who understand and respect your feelings.

Seek Support: Consider joining a support group or talking to a therapist who specialises in grief and loss. Connecting with others who have experienced similar situations can provide valuable support and understanding.

Keep in mind that not everyone may understand or be sensitive to your situation. Some people may ask the question casually without realising the potential impact it may have. It's okay to educate others about your experience if you feel comfortable doing so, but you are not obligated to disclose more than you're comfortable with.

It's also important to acknowledge that your feelings may change over time. What feels right for you to share in one moment may not feel the same in another. Give yourself permission to adapt your responses based on your current emotional state and needs.

BEING AROUND BABIES

Being around babies after experiencing a loss can evoke a range of emotions, from tender longing to profound sadness. Here are some reflections on navigating this delicate experience:

Mixed Emotions: Being around babies after a loss can stir up a complex mix of emotions. While you may feel joy and warmth in the presence of babies, you may also experience feelings of grief, longing, and even jealousy. It's normal to have conflicting emotions, and it's important to be gentle with yourself as you navigate them.

Triggers and Reminders: Seeing babies who are around the same age as the age your baby would be can serve as potent reminders of your own loss. Certain sights, sounds, or gestures may trigger memories and emotions, catching you off guard. It's essential to acknowledge these triggers and allow yourself to feel whatever comes up without judgment.

Guilt and Shame: It's common to experience feelings of guilt or shame for having negative emotions around babies, especially if they belong to friends or family members. Remember that your feelings are valid, and it's okay to prioritise your own emotional well-being. Seek support from understanding loved ones who can offer empathy and reassurance.

Setting Boundaries: It's important to set boundaries and communicate your needs when it comes to interacting with babies after a loss. If you need some space or if certain situations feel too overwhelming, don't hesitate to speak up and take care of yourself. True friends and family will understand and respect your boundaries.

Honouring Your Baby's Memory: Being around babies can also provide opportunities to honour the memory of the child you lost. You may find comfort in participating in activities or rituals that allow you to remember and celebrate your baby's life, such as creating keepsakes or sharing stories with loved ones.

Seeking Support: Don't hesitate to reach out for support from others who have experienced similar losses. Connecting with support groups or seeking guidance from a therapist who specialises in grief and loss can provide valuable validation and understanding during this challenging time.

Ultimately, navigating the experience of being around babies after baby loss is deeply personal and unique to each individual. Be patient with yourself as you navigate these emotions, and remember that healing takes time. You are not alone, and there is support available to help you through this journey.

Welcoming my niece into the world just over a month before Matthew's arrival brought a cascade of emotions within me - jealousy, as I witnessed the joy surrounding her birth; joy, as I celebrated her new life; grief, as I grappled with my own loss; and longing, as I yearned for moments with Matthew that would never come to be. These feelings are a natural part of the complex tapestry of human emotions.

There were moments when I found myself yearning to spend time with my niece, craving the innocent joy and newness that she brought into our lives. Yet, there were also times when the ache of loss made it almost unbearable to be around her, a reminder of the moments I would never share with Matthew.

By communicating openly with others about my experiences, I found a sense of understanding and support that helped me on my journey of healing.

Use these pages to write about how you feel when around other babies.

PREGNANT FRIENDS AND FAMILY

Being around pregnant friends and family members after experiencing a loss can be a deeply emotional journey, marked by a complex tapestry of feelings.

It's a delicate balance between joy for their new chapter and the ache of your own loss.

Every baby bump, every excited announcement, and every nursery decoration can serve as reminders of the dreams you once held and the little one you long to hold again. It's natural to feel a mix of happiness and sadness, hope and grief, as you navigate this emotional landscape.

There may be moments when you feel overwhelmed by the flood of emotions, wishing for the chance to share in the joy without the shadow of your loss. It's okay to take a step back and honor your feelings, allowing yourself the space to process and heal.

At the same time, being around pregnant loved ones can also offer moments of connection and shared understanding. They may not fully grasp the depth of your sorrow, but their empathy and support can serve as a source of comfort along the way.

Remember, it's okay to set boundaries and prioritise your own well-being. Whether that means opting out of baby-related events when it feels too overwhelming or seeking support from understanding friends and family members, do what feels right for you.

Your pregnant friend or family member will be acutely aware of the loss of your precious little one. They will be aware that the thought of their pregnancy journey is possibly stirring up painful memories for you. They want to share their happiness with you, yet they are mindful of your emotions.

Above all, be gentle with yourself as you navigate this complex journey. Your feelings are valid, and it's important to honor them as you continue to heal and find moments of peace amidst the storm. You are not alone, and there is love and support surrounding you, even in the midst of your grief.

How quietly you tiptoed
into our world,
almost silently,
only for a moment you
stayed … but what an
imprint your footprints
have left upon our
hearts.

DOROTHY FERGUSON

**Write a poem in memory
of your little one.**

I carried you every
second of your life
and
I will love you every
second of mine.

UNKNOWN

Write about the things you are looking forward to.

HAS EVERYONE FORGOTTEN AND MOVED ON?

Feeling like everyone has forgotten and moved on after experiencing the loss of a baby can be an incredibly lonely and isolating experience.

In the immediate aftermath of loss, there's often an outpouring of support and sympathy from friends and family. But as time passes and life continues, it can feel like the world around you has moved on while you're left behind in a sea of grief.

You might notice that conversations with friends become less frequent, and invitations to social gatherings dwindle. People may hesitate to bring up your loss, fearing that they'll remind you of your pain or say the wrong thing. But in their silence, it can feel like your baby's memory is fading away, becoming a distant echo in a world that's moved on.

Meanwhile, you're still grappling with the raw ache of your loss every day. The empty nursery, the unopened baby gifts, and the milestones that will never be reached serve as constant reminders of the child you loved and lost. And as time goes on, the fear of being forgotten becomes a heavy burden to bear.

Amidst the loneliness and despair, it's important to remember that your baby's memory lives on in your heart. Your grief is valid, and your baby's life mattered. It's okay to reach out to loved ones and share your feelings, even if it feels like they've moved on. And if you find that you need additional support, there are counsellors, support groups, and online communities filled with people who understand what you're going through.

In time, you may find that the pain of your loss doesn't lessen, but it does become more manageable. And though it may feel like the world has forgotten, know that your baby's memory will always be cherished, and your love for them will never fade.

Use this space to record your feelings and why you feel everyone has moved on.

Farewell Little One

In the gentle embrace of starlit skies,
My precious one, it's time to say goodbye.
Though your time with me was far too brief,
Your love and light bring solace beyond belief.

In whispered dreams, you'll forever dwell,
A cherished memory, no words can tell.
Your tiny presence, a beacon of grace,
In my heart, you'll always have a place.

Though tears may fall like gentle rain,
Your spirit lingers, easing the pain.
In the quiet whispers of the night,
I'll hold you close, my guiding light.

So rest now, my sweet angel, in peaceful sleep,
As into the starry heavens, your love I'll keep.
Though parted by fate's unyielding hand,
In my heart, you'll forever stand.

UNKNOWN

YOUR STORY
Use these next few pages to write your story. Whatever comes into your head, whatever your thoughts.

Self-Compassion: Explore your feelings towards yourself during this time. How have you shown yourself compassion and kindness?

HAVING ANOTHER BABY

In the midst of grief, the thought of welcoming another baby into your lives can feel both daunting and hopeful.

It's a journey fraught with mixed emotions—a delicate balance between honouring the precious memories of the baby you have lost and embracing the possibility of new life.

For some, the decision to try again is immediate, driven by an unwavering desire to expand their family despite the pain of loss. For others, it's a journey marked by hesitation and uncertainty.

Each person's journey is unique, shaped by their own experiences and emotions. There's no right or wrong timeline for deciding to have another baby—only what feels right for the individual or couple as they navigate the delicate balance between past sorrow and future possibilities.

For some individuals or couples, the decision not to try for another baby after experiencing loss is a deeply personal one, rooted in a multitude of factors. They may find solace in their existing family dynamic or feel content with the children they already have.

Others may grapple with the fear of facing another loss or simply feel that they have reached a point of closure in their journey towards parenthood. Whatever the reasons may be, choosing not to pursue another pregnancy is a valid and respectable choice—one that reflects their unique circumstances, emotions, and needs.

As you embark on this journey, you will carry with you the love and memories of the baby you lost, their presence woven into the fabric of your family's story.

write about your thoughts and feelings about having another baby.

FOREVER REMEMBERED

Years may pass, but the memory of your baby will remain etched in your heart. It's okay to talk about your little one, even as time marches on. In fact, sharing memories and stories can be a powerful way to keep their spirit alive and honour the impact they had on your life.

These conversations allow us to reminisce about the precious moments we shared, the dreams we held, and the love that continues to endure. While the pain of loss may never fully fade, talking about our babies years later helps ensure that they are never forgotten—that their presence, however brief, continues to shape and enrich our lives in meaningful ways.

As the years go by, the void left by a lost baby may evolve, but it never truly disappears. It's natural to want to keep their memory alive, to speak their name and share their story, even long after they're gone. These conversations serve as a testament to the enduring love we hold for our little ones and the profound impact they had on our lives. They remind us that their existence, however fleeting, mattered deeply and that they will always hold a special place in our hearts. So, don't hesitate to talk about your lost baby, even years down the road. They may not be here with us, but they will never be forgotten.

Matthew's Story

I want to offer you some reassurance: over time, the pain may lessen, but I want to be completely transparent with you. What has happened will stay with you, etched into your memory with vivid clarity.

I want to share Matthew's story with you. Yes It is 34 years ago, but as you will read, those memories are still engraved within my heart.

Sitting down in a room, we were informed of the necessity for an emergency C-section to give "the baby" any chance of survival. At 28 weeks, preparations for the worst were underway. Upon waking from the anesthesia, I was relieved to hear that Matthew had made it to the neonatal unit, and in my mind having made it that far he was going to be fine. However, nothing could have prepared my young 20-year-old self for what I encountered when I was wheeled into the unit to meet him: his fragile appearance, the web of wires, the constant beeping of machinery, and the nurses tirelessly working to sustain his breath and life. My perfect little boy weighing 2lb 13oz, with noteably long fingers like his mummy.

The two days of his life were spent in the unit only able to touch him through the holes of the incubator. He was operated on as his lungs were sticking together so they had to make small holes to try and help his fragile body.

Then, the most agonising conversation unfolded - we were informed that all options had been exhausted, and at this juncture, it was highly probable that he would suffer brain damage, with the ventilator serving as his sole lifeline. They requested our consent to discontinue life support. Affixing my signature to grant permission remains, and will always be, the most difficult task I've ever faced in my life.

Before Matthew was taken out of the incubator, he was baptised, a short but meaningful ceremony. Not long after, Matthew was placed in my arms as he took his final breaths, tears streaming down my face as if they would never cease. After a brief moment, the nurse examined him and softly uttered, "he has passed."

"He has passed" The words, I was dreading. For a moment, I didn't believe, this wasn't what was supposed to happen. A sound escaped me as I struggled to comprehend. I remained seated, feeling like an eternity passed before they gently took him away. All I wanted was to hold him close and never let him go.

I returned to my bed, consumed by a sense of emptiness. It seemed there was a shift change for the nurses. I lay there, tears streaming down my face, when a nurse entered and enquired about my distress, dismissing it as mere hormonal fluctuations. I longed to unleash my anguish upon her, to articulate the depth of my pain, but the words remained trapped as I continued to weep.

The sound of newborns crying in the ward felt cruel. I felt torn - I didn't want to remain in that hospital, yet I couldn't bear the thought of leaving without Matthew.

Later in the day, we found solace in a peaceful room where we could spend precious moments with Matthew.

The nurses had lovingly dressed him for the first time and placed him in a Moses basket, making him appear as if he were peacefully sleeping.

Clad in a white onesie and a lemon cardigan, he looked angelic. The nurse gave me a lock of Matthews hair and offered to take photographs, which we accepted. Polaroid snapshots captured the bittersweet moments as we held him close. I expressed my heartfelt farewell, promising him that he would always be remembered and loved dearly.

Due to the necessity of the C-section, I was required to stay in the hospital for a few more days. During this time, I felt adrift, consumed by anger and bitterness, and found myself lashing out. I experienced a whirlwind of emotions, processing every feeling imaginable.

Matthew's father has remained a shadowy figure in my narrative until now. He was not a source of comfort or understanding; instead, he embodied traits of cruelty and indifference, which I did know he had a tendency to.

Despite the toxicity of our relationship, he was, in a twisted sense, all that tethered me to Matthew's existence. In my desperation for solace and shared understanding, I found myself seeking his support, believing, perhaps naively, that he might be the only one who truly comprehended the depth of my emotional turmoil.

The moment arrived to depart from the hospital, leaving behind its walls empty-handed, and that sensation has remained etched within me, unfading with time. Departing from the hospital felt like the final page of a chapter turning, leaving the impression that once we stepped outside its walls, it would be as if Matthew had never existed.

Certainly, this notion was far from the truth; Matthew would forever reside in my memories and within the depths of my heart.

Facing the prospect of re-entering the real world, I was overwhelmed with fear. I no longer felt whole; a sense of incompleteness enveloped me.

As days turned into weeks, I found myself grappling with the absence of support from Matthew's father. While I navigated my grief, it appeared as though he scarcely acknowledged the loss. Instead, his aggression towards me intensified, casting a shadow over my already tumultuous journey. The escalation of threats against my life, alongside physical assaults, culminated in his arrest.

These public displays of violence and intimidation underscored the urgency of the situation.

I summoned the courage to forge ahead alone, recognising that his presence had transformed into a grave threat, not only to myself but to those around me. Knowing that he had a history of violent crimes further validated my decision to leave him.

It was in making that decsion that I truly found the strength to start to learn to live again and move forwards.

In the wake of unimaginable loss, I find myself grappling with the inexplicable twists of fate. My son Matthew, just a baby, departed from this world far too soon. Yet, amid the echoes of grief, a haunting thought emerges. Could his passing have been a twist of fate, a merciful escape from the clutches of his violent father? It's a notion that bends the mind and pierces the heart, yet offers a fragile thread of consolation amidst the anguish.

Life alongside Matthew's father was a fragile existence, and would inevitably hurtle towards a dark and tragic outcome. Escaping from that environment was the only viable solution to ensure safety and well-being.

A JOURNEY TO FREEDOM

In my quiet moments, I found my inner power,
Leaving behind the dark, I took it hour by hour.
Guided by what I knew, I found my way out,
Escaping from the violence, I faced without doubt.

As the truth unfolded, his wrongs came to light,
It was clear leaving was wise, it felt right.
Every move I made showed I was strong,
Leaving shadows behind, I chose where I belong.
In Matthew's memory, I found my rightful place.

Tiny Light

In the quiet of the night,
A tiny light flickers bright.
Though gone too soon,
you'll always stay,
In our hearts, you light the way.

UNKNOWN

MATTHEW'S ETERNAL LIGHT

In your two days, a lifetime's love,
Matthew, my angel, sent from above.
Though brief your stay, your presence bright,
In my heart, you'll forever ignite.

Rest now, dear Matthew, in heaven's embrace,
Your spirit lives on, a timeless trace.
In my dreams, you'll forever reside,
My precious son, my eternal guide.

Reflect on any questions or uncertainties you may have about your loss. What do you wish you understood better?

Think about who you can talk with, whether there are any groups that may be able to help you with these uncertainties.

Matthew

May the stars whisper your name softly as you slumber, keeping watch until we're together again.
God Bless
Love Mummy xxx

KEEPING BABY'S MEMORY ALIVE

Your baby loss book is more than just ink on paper; it's a sanctuary of memories, a testament to a love that transcends time.

As you close its covers, you don't lock away the pain of loss; instead, you embrace the comfort it offers. In the days ahead, you'll find yourself drawn to its pages, seeking solace in the mementos, the words that capture your journey together. Each moment you spend revisiting those pages is a gentle reminder that your baby's memory lives on.

This book isn't just a keepsake; it's a lifeline. When grief threatens to overwhelm you, you'll turn to its familiar pages, finding strength in the shared moments of joy and sorrow. It's a tangible link to the love you'll always carry in your heart, a beacon of hope in your darkest hours.

So hold onto this precious gift, knowing that in keeping your baby's memory alive, you keep their love alive too. As you turn its pages, you'll find comfort in the knowledge that your baby will always be with you, their spirit guiding you with a love that knows no end.

Use the following pages to write about anything that is in your heart. Continue writing for as long as you need to.

HELP AND SUPPORT

In the UK, there are several organisations that offer support to individuals and families who have experienced baby loss. Some of these organisations include:

SANDS (Stillbirth and Neonatal Death Society)
SANDS is a UK charity that provides support to anyone affected by the death of a baby during pregnancy, at birth, or shortly after. They offer a range of services, including helplines, support groups, online forums, and information resources.

Tommy's
Tommy's is a charity that funds research into miscarriage, stillbirth, and premature birth, and provides support to families affected by these issues. They offer a range of support services, including a helpline, online support groups, information resources, and research initiatives.

Miscarriage Association
The Miscarriage Association is a charity that provides support and information to anyone affected by miscarriage, ectopic pregnancy, or molar pregnancy. They offer a helpline, online support forums, information leaflets, and support groups across the UK.

Child Bereavement UK
Child Bereavement UK provides support to families and professionals dealing with the loss of a child of any age, including babies. They offer a helpline, support groups, counseling services, and training for professionals.

Bliss
Bliss is a charity that provides support to families of premature and sick babies. While their focus is primarily on supporting families with babies in neonatal care, they also offer support to families who have experienced the loss of a baby.

These organisations offer valuable support and resources to individuals and families coping with baby loss in the UK. Reaching out to one of these organisations can provide much-needed support and guidance during this difficult time.

You may also find support from baby loss social media groups such as Stillbirth and Infant Loss Support Group on Facebook.

SPECIAL THANKS TO DEB

In the pages of this book, there's a special space reserved for thanks —a space dedicated to someone whose simple idea sparked a flame of inspiration in my heart. Deb, your suggestion illuminated a path that I had not yet considered, guiding me towards a deeper understanding of my own journey through baby loss.

Your words inspired me to put pen to paper, to share parts of my journey with others, and to shine a light on the often silent struggles of baby loss.

Your idea not only inspired this book but also reminded me of the power of connection—the power of reaching out to others in times of need, and the profound impact that a simple gesture of kindness can have on someone's life.

So, I extend my thanks to you, Deb. Your idea sparked a journey that has touched my soul in ways I never imagined, and for that, I am forever grateful.

SPECIAL GRATITUDE TO:

My Husband, Neil, for his unwavering support of my decision to pen this book and for his efforts in raising funds for SANDS in memory of my son Matthew.

Owen, my son, who proudly bears Matthew as his middle name.

My resilient daughter, Lucy, who also entered this world prematurely, yet filled it with her strength and light.

Printed in Great Britain
by Amazon